GW00602780

Other giftbooks in this series

Birthday Girl!

Sorry

Little things mean a lot

Go Girl!

I love you madly

Published simultaneously in 2007 by Helen Exley Giftbooks in Great Britain and Helen Exley Giftbooks LLC in the USA.

12 11 10 9 8 7 6 5 4 3 2

ISBN 13: 978-1-84634-088-8

A copy of the CIP data is available from the British Library on request.

Words by Stuart and Linda Macfarlane
Edited by Helen Exley
Pictures by Roger Greenhough and Caroline Gardner
Printed in China

Helen Exley Giftbooks, 16 Chalk Hill, Watford, Herts WD19 4BG, UK
www.helenexleygiftbooks.com

Birthday Boy!

By Stuart &
Linda Macfarlane

A HELEN EXLEY
GIFTBOOK

ZZZZzzzz .....

Wakening....

Time check....

Ten past midnight....

Yip! Time to get up!!

Just Another Day?

A day older.

Birthday!

A year older!

Yippeeeeeeee!!!!

Presents to open.

Cake to eat.

Balloons to burst.

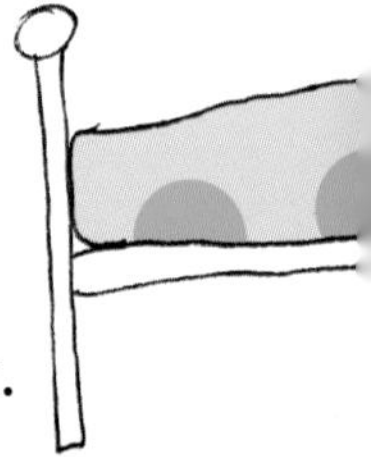

You wake with a start,
realising it's your birthday. Grin.
Normally you would go
straight back to sleep but today
is special – there are gifts to open,

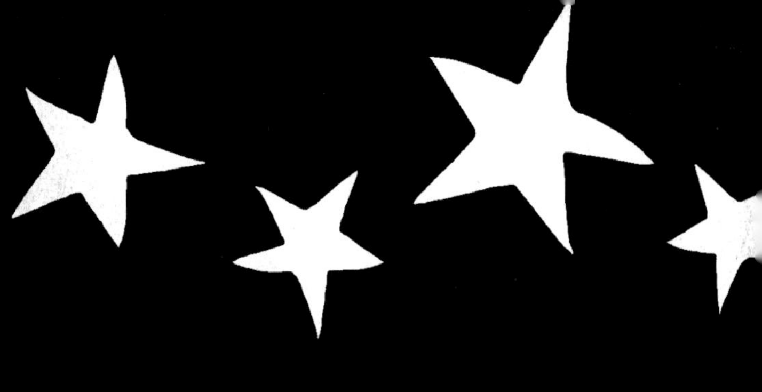

cake to eat and
a huge birthday party to enjoy.
And the fact that it
is just past midnight
isn't going to delay the fun!

Good morning!
Happy Birthday!
The moment you have
waited 364 days for
has finally arrived.

Not a second to waste! Get out of bed

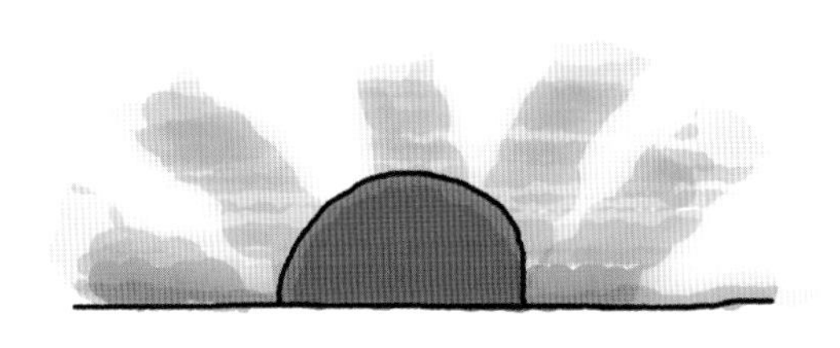

It's your birthday – a day for FUN!

Ring the bell,
Bang the gong,
Beat the drum,
Sound the horn,
It's your birthday.

Whether eight or eighty,
king or pauper,
schoolboy or
rocket scientist,
everyone
loves their birthday.

Fantastic!

Amazing!

Outstanding!

Stupendous

Incredible!

Wonderful!

Superb!

Exciting!

Tremendous!

Spectacular!

Brilliant!

I hope your day will be ALL of these.

Hinting about
what gifts you want:
Send an email – every ten minutes.
Have an airplane tow a
banner across the sky.
Create the website
www.what-to-buy-me.com

t ideas under doormat

Many happy returns.
With each birthday I wish you
greater love, greater happiness...
and a greater number of gifts!

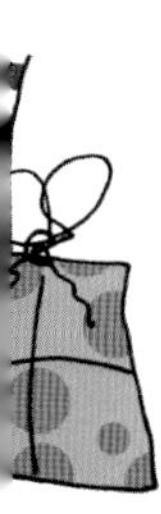

If I had a wish
I would give to you;
The brightest star in the sky.
An ocean full of dolphins and whales.
A desert that stretches for
ten thousand miles.
You are such a wonderful person,
nothing in your life
should ever be ordinary.
And you are such a wonderful person,
everything in your life
should be spectacular.

May your
birthday be a day
to remember.
A day blessed
with love, fun
and joy.

Today you
must laugh and dance
and sing and only do the
things you really enjoy.

I hope your birthday,
sparkles, shimmers
and goes off
with a bang!

Make the most of
every moment of this day.
Have the craziest,
happiest time ever.

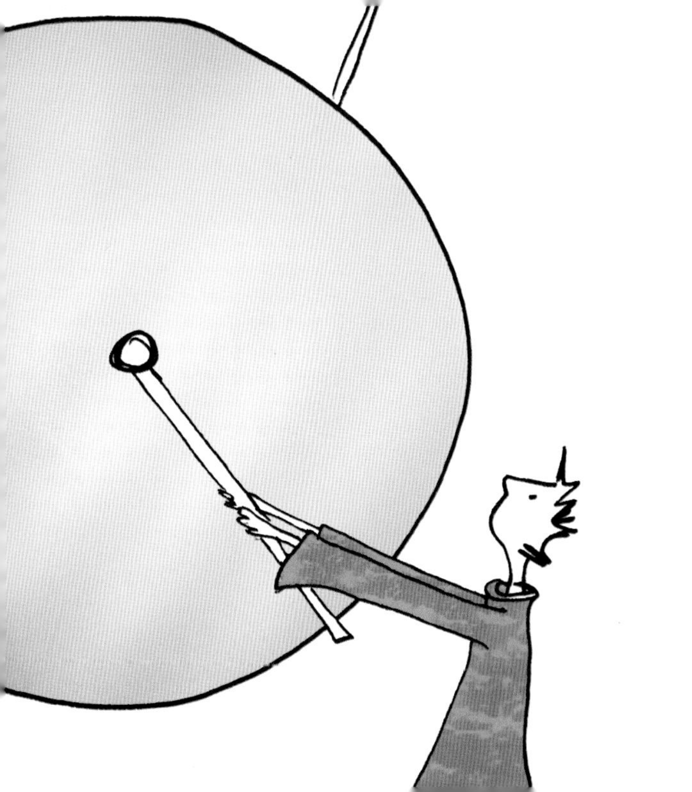

Many happy returns
to you on this special day.
But more importantly,
may you be blessed
with happiness,
today and every day.

A birthday is
a perfect excuse
for wearing
something really silly.

Dance today.

Sing today.

Abandon all care.

Forget all work.

This is a time

for rapturous revelry.

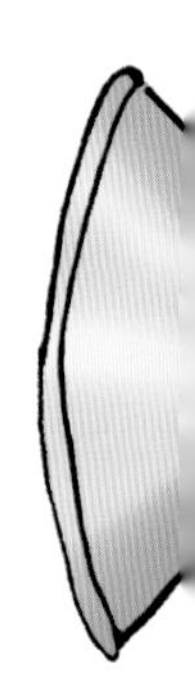

In the hullabaloo
of your birthday celebrations
take a few moments to
look back on the year
and feel proud of
everything you have done.

A Happy Birthday is...

being with friends.

A Happy Birthday is...
using your birthday money
to buy drums! Drums to
drive everyone crazy.

Birthday:
The one day when it's
definitely better to
receive than to give.

The worst birthday presents ever!!!

Cuddly soft toys.

Socks that are four sizes too small –

in fact any socks!

A pink top with one sleeve too long.

Soppy poetry books.

Smelly stuff to put in the bath. Flowers.

The bestseller,

"Get in touch with your sensitive side."

What I dreamed of getting.

What I got.

A ride on a helicopter.

A plastic plane.

A trip to Disneyland.

A trip to the dentist.

A top-of-the-range computer.

A plastic abacus.

My own Porsche.

To wash the car.

Murphy's Birthday Laws:

What can go wrong will go wrong!!

You will sleep in and miss your birthday completely.

Your surprise party will be such a surprise that no one turns up.

The candles will set fire to your cake.

Your twin will forget it's your birthday.

The day will be cancelled!

The best present
isn't necessarily something
very expensive –
often a simple gift
given with love and consideration
outshines all the others.

A Happy Birthday is...
being surrounded by love.

The best bit
about getting older
is that each year the cake
needs to be bigger than the last
to take the increasing number of candles.

May your biggest
and best gift
be lots and lots and lots
of happiness.

Fun Time!

A birthday is a time for fun,
Forgetting all your troubles,
So skip, hop, leap and jump,
And blow some massive bubbles,
A birthday is a time for joy,
So this is what to do,
Spin around a dozen times,
And pointlessly shout yahoooooo!

PARTY RULES

* Invite everyone you know and many you don't know.
* Evacuate the rest of the street.
* Have enough food and drink to feed a small nation.
* Music should be played at 7.5 on the Richter Scale.
* Remove all clocks and watches – let the party rock forever.
* Have pre-planned excuses to counter complaints from the street committee, riot police and the army.

Go wild on your birthday –
gorge yourself with cake and
masses of ice cream.
Leave being sensible till
your next birthday.

The party is over.
All the food has been eaten.
All the presents opened.
The weary birthday bloke flops down.
It has been the best birthday
ever but, in a funny sort of way,
you're glad it's over –
now you can start looking forward
to your next birthday.

Only with age
comes true wisdom –
so any day now
you could have
a smart idea.

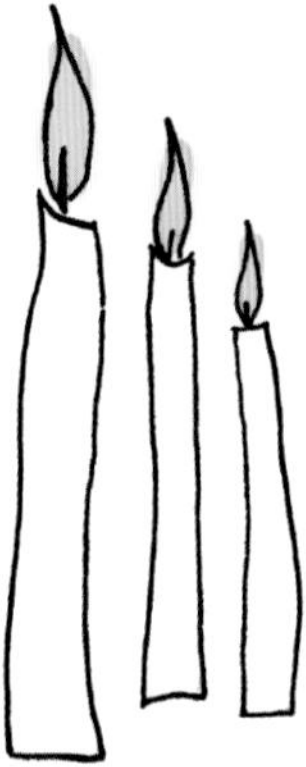

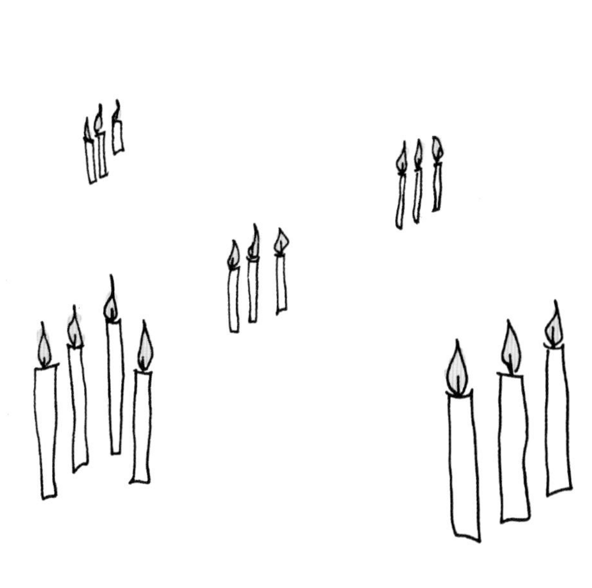

As you get older you become wiser. At any moment intelligent thoughts can pop into your head. As a result you will consider becoming a philosopher or great genius. Don't worry. The disagreeable intelligent thoughts will soon disappear and normality will resume.

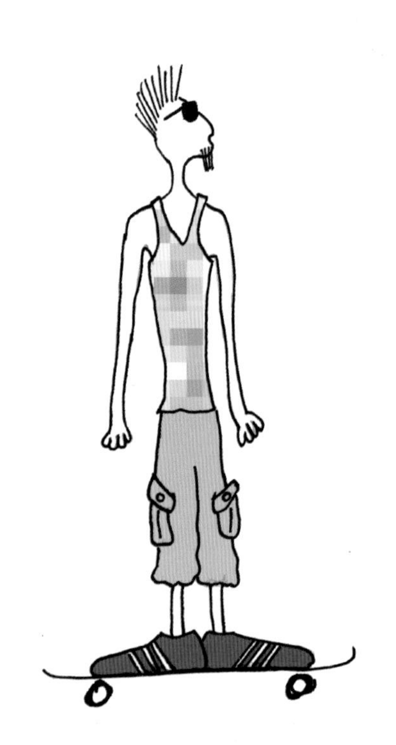

The best part of a birthday
is the end of the day when you can stand
quietly and think about all the
wonderful presents you received
and all the fun you had
with your friends.

It's a tragedy!
It's a disaster!
It's a sad, sad fact!
It will not be your birthday,
For another
three-hundred-and-sixty-four days.

May your life be one long,
happy birthday party.

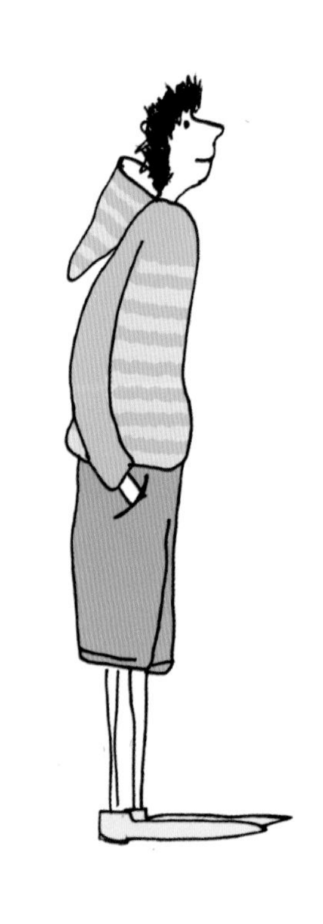

May your year be
filled with rainbow days.

Helen Exley runs her own publishing company
which sells giftbooks in more than seventy countries.
Helen's books cover the many events and emotions in life,
and she was eager to produce a book to say a simple 'sorry'.
Caroline Gardner's delightfully quirky 'elfin' cards
provided the inspiration Helen needed to go ahead
with this idea, and from there this series of stylish
and witty books quickly grew.

Caroline Gardner Publishing has been producing beautifully
designed stationery from offices overlooking the River Thames
in England since 1993 and has been developing the distinctive
'elfin' stationery range over the last five years.
There are also several new illustrations created especially for
these books by artist Roger Greenhough.

Stuart and Linda Macfarlane live in Glasgow, Scotland.
They have produced several books with Helen Exley
including *The Little Book of Stress*, *Old Wrecks' Jokes*,
and the hugely successful *Utterly adorable cats*.